Mel Bay's
FIDDLE TUNES & IRISH MUSIC FOR MANDOLIN

By Dan Gelo

SIXTY-TWO TUNES AND INSTRUCTION FOR THE INTERMEDIATE AND ADVANCED PLAYER

1 2 3 4 5 6 7 8 9 0

CONTENTS

For Gabrielle

Special thanks to: Rich and Stef Stillman, Eugene Ettore,
John Pariso, Gene Lowinger and my parents, Joseph and Catherine Gelo.

4

Introduction

The mandolin is the smallest member of the lute family
of stringed instruments. Several kinds of mandolins, each
with a different number of strings, evolved in the city-states
of Renaissance Italy. The Neapolitan version, with four
pairs of strings tuned like a violin, superceded the other
varieties in popularity. The mandolin was adopted as a folk
instrument throughout Europe, from Russia to England. It
also enjoyed the attention of classical musicians, and
Beethoven, Mozart and Hummel, among others, composed for
mandolin.

The mandolin came into use in Irish and American folk
music during the nineteenth century. Irish seafarers brought
home mandolins from southern Europe. American farmers ordered
them through mail order catalogues. The conservative Irish were
slow to accept the mandolin, and the best Irish players
have only recently gained recognition within their tradition.
In America the mandolin became established more quickly; by
the 1920's it was being featured in fiddle bands like Gid
Tanner's Skillet Lickers and later by Bill Monroe, the father
of bluegrass music.

Today it is likely that any well-rounded mandolinist you meet
will have some fiddle tunes in his repertoire. The
mandolin and violin are related by the fact that they share
the same tuning, so it is easy to understand how fiddle tunes

came to be played on the mandolin. Indeed, fiddle tunes are
also performed on guitar, banjo, flute, tin whistle, accordion,
seemingly any instrument with melodic capabilities. But only
the mandolinist can borrow certain fingerings and techniques
directly from the fiddler. Other times, of course, even the
mandolinist must accomodate the tune to his own instrument.
Discovering fiddle tunes from different traditions and
performing them on mandolin is a rewarding end in itself.
Not only are these melodies beautiful and inspiring, but
they develop techniques that the mandolinist can apply to
other types of music as well. Most important, perhaps, fiddle
tunes are just _fun_ to play.

This book can show you certain techniques and introduce
you to a wealth of fine music, but it is not a substitute
for experience. To be a part of the tradition you need to
play with other musicians, and more importantly, listen
to other musicians, live and on record. A recommended disco-
graphy appears at the end of this book.
So many of the tunes in this book bring me memories of
great friends and good times, and I hope that as time passes,
they will do the same for you.

Technique and Ornamentation

When a good fiddler or mandolinist plays a tune, he individualizes it and leaves his signature upon it, so to speak. This is accomplished by adding subtle variation to the basic melody. Some of these variations have been standardized for the fiddle; they are called ornaments. When and when not to use ornaments is a personal choice and allows for creativity. The tunes in this collection have ornaments written in, so that you will learn to execute them and get some ideas about where to place them. Some mandolin ornaments, like the picked triplet, have been borrowed from the fiddle. Other techniques, like the hammer-on, are peculiar to fretted instruments.

The Left Hand

Most ornaments in fiddle music are sounded with the left hand. Proper left hand positioning is essential, so let's get back to basics for a moment:

1. Arch your left wrist away from your body so that the palm of your hand does not press against the neck of the mandolin.

2. Your thumb should not hook around the neck for support, it should be placed behind the neck.

3. Your fingers should be arched over the fingerboard, not flat.

4. For the best tone, fret close to the frets with the tips of your fingers.

5. Remember, economy of motion is important. The best players are the ones that make it look easy, not hard, so avoid unnecessary or exaggerated finger movements.

Left Hand Techniques

It is possible to fret a string so hard that you produce a

note. This is called a <u>hammer</u>-<u>on</u>. Pick an open or fretted

note with the right hand, then slam down your finger on the

next desired note.

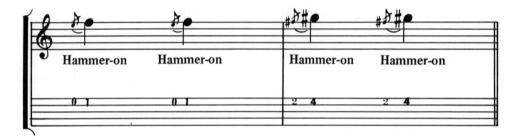

Try these hammers on all four strings.

A <u>pull</u>-<u>off</u> works the opposite of a hammer-on. A fretted note

is picked with the right hand, and the next note is sounded

by plucking the string with a left-hand finger.

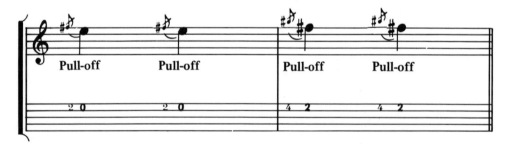

Classical violinists call the pull-off "left-hand pizzicato."

Traditional fiddlers seldom use this technique, but it works

well on the mandolin.

It is also possible to fret and pick a note, then slide your left-hand finger up to the next note. <u>Slides</u> are used commonly by American fiddlers, and occasionally by Irish players.

Slides can be exaggerated: or quick:

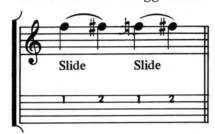 

After you feel comfortable with the hammer-on, pull-off, and slide, try to recognize the situations in which they occur.

For instance, slides are often used to sound single grace notes:

Pull-offs occur on single grace notes and sixteenth notes:

Hammer-ons are good for sounding double grace notes:

or, they can be used along with pull-offs to sound triplets:

In all cases, the notes which the ornament applies to are connected by a tie line ⌒.

Harmonics are used on a few of the tunes. If you touch a string lightly with the fourth finger of your left hand directly over the twelfth fret, and pick the string, you will get a pleasant "chime" sound. What you are doing is causing the string to vibrate in two equal halves, one on each side of the twelfth fret. This allows the overtones, or harmonics, to ring. Harmonics add a nice touch at the end of a tune or measure. They are written:

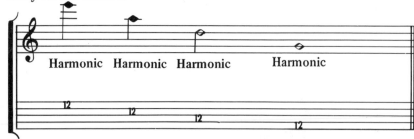

Other harmonics can be found at the seventh and fifth frets. Experiment!

10

The Right Hand

Right hand dexterity is all-important, but it is not achieved

overnight. Here are some points to consider:

1. Learn a new tune by playing it slowly, so that the notes
   are sounded evenly and cleanly. Your speed will increase
   automatically as you become familiar with the tune.

2. The picking motion should come mostly from your wrist,
   rather than from your elbow or shoulder. Concentrate
   on keeping your wrist loose.

3. Hold the pick firmly but don't squeeze it; squeezing the
   pick will actually cause your wrist to tighten up.

4. Most good mandolin players lightly rest their third and
   fourth fingers on the pickguard for extra stability.

5. Try using a medium pick. Thin picks flex too much and
   make your wrist work overtime, plus they tend to produce
   a slappy tone. Those heavy picks popular with today's
   bluegrass mandolinists are really too stiff for playing
   the rapid triplets in some Irish tunes.

6. For maximum volume and to avoid that scratchy feeling,
   make sure that the pick strikes the strings squarely.
   Check your pick for signs of wear; uneven wear on one
   edge means that the pick is hitting the strings at an
   angle.

Right Hand Techniques

For the sake of clarity, up and down picking strokes are not
indicated in the music except for a few extra-tricky passages,
in which case the symbols ⊓ (down stroke) and ⋁ (up stroke)
appear above the notes.

A general rule to follow is this: use down strokes on all notes
except for eighth notes and sixteenth notes. Where these
occur, pick down, up, down, up etc. <u>Always</u> begin a measure
or a group of eighth or sixteenth notes with a downstroke,
unless otherwise indicated. An application of this rule
would look like this:

Work to get a smooth, even back-and-forth motion on the eighth
and sixteenth notes.

<u>Tremolo</u> can be applied when you want to sustain a note.
Tremolo is the rapid back-and-forth motion of the pick.
Tremoloed notes are indicated by two diagonal slashes beneath
the note head ♩ . Try this excercise (with your wrist loose!)
for building a rapid tremolo:

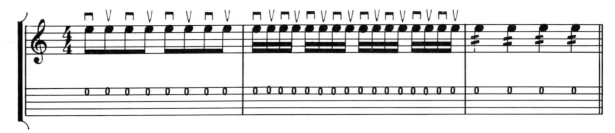

Tremolo seems to work particularly well on the slow tunes and waltzes. Feel free to try it in different places; my tremolo marks are merely suggestions.

There is only one true ornament that is played with the right hand, and that is the <u>picked triplet.</u> Mandolinists borrow this idea from the fiddler's bowed triplet. It looks like this:

A few of the tunes use a technique known as <u>crosspicking.</u> Crosspicking sounds complicated, but it is simply a predetermined right hand picking pattern. Try this basic pattern:

Often found in combination with alternating strokes:

Familiarize yourself with these patterns now, and the cross-picked tunes will be much easier to learn.

An arpeggio, or broken chord, creates a sound reminiscent
of the Irish harp. The harp effect requires that you play the
notes of a three- or four-note chord one at a time, in quick
succession, with a downward brushing motion. Chords played
in this manner use this symbol: ⦙ .

Bear in mind that all these techniques are like spices;
if you use them sparingly they will add flavor to some al-
ready beautiful melodies. But to use them too much, with no
thought or feeling, is definitely bad taste!

Accompaniment

Most Irish musicians are quite happy to play melodies without any chordal accompaniment and a group of Irish instrumentalists will usually all play the melody of a piece simultaneously. You must remember that chordal harmony is a relatively recent development in the history of western music, and Irish fiddle tunes have an ancient ancestry. The mandolinist might wish to play chords on the American tunes, however, because American players usually alternate between playing melodic "breaks" and then playing chords while someone else takes a "break." The Irish tunes also sound good when played in this manner. Chords have been provided for all of the tunes.

There are two manners of playing chords, both using <u>only</u> <u>down</u> strokes. The first method is <u>brush</u> down on <u>open</u> chords on the <u>strong</u> beats of the measure:

The second method is to <u>chop</u> down on <u>closed</u> chords on the <u>weak</u> beats of the measure:

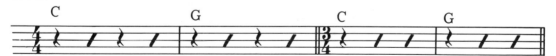

Remember, use only down strokes. Up strokes sound slappy and detract from the rhythm.

The <u>brush</u> method works best for slow tunes and Irish tunes, while the <u>chop</u> method seems best for American tunes and fast playing, but these are general rules and you should experiment and discover your own preferences.

15

Types of Fiddle Tunes

Fiddle tunes are classified according to their time signatures

and according to what dance steps are used with them. It

is helpful to know the different categories; for instance

if someone says "jig" you can anticipate a moderate or fast

tune in 6/8 time. Here are the different tune types and

characteristics:

reel-in 2/4 or 4/4 time; appears throughout Britain and
Anglo-America. The reel is the most popular and widespread
tune form. The Irish play reels very quickly and with a
lot of ornamentation, while the Scottish and Americans play
them a little more slowly and simply.

strathspey- a slow type of reel that developed near the Spey
River, northeastern Scotland. Strathspeys have a characteristic
dotted rhythm ♩♪♪♩. They are seldom heard outside of Scotland,
Shetland, and Cape Breton.

breakdown- in 2/4 or 4/4 time; a fast, driving American
tune. Breakdown melodies are often derived from older Scottish
reels.

hornpipe- in 2/4 or 4/4 time; a slower, jauntier melody
distinguishes the hornpipe from the reel. The hornpipe is
correctly played, though not notated, with a bounce, so that
notes like this ♫ ♫ actually sound more like this ♪♪ ♪♪ .
Hornpipes probably originated in England and are now played
throughout Britain, Canada and the northern U.S.

jig- in 6/8 time; most jigs are Irish or English in origin;
now they occur in Scotland, Canada and New England as well.
In the southern and western U.S., dances in 6/8 time are
rare, so jigs are seldom played in these regions. Moderate
or fast tempo.

slip jig- in 9/8 time; sometimes called "hop jig", no doubt
because the dancer would leap at certain points in the tune.
Slip jigs are widespread in the British Isles but rare in
American and Canadian tradition. Again, moderate or fast
tempo.

planxty- in Ireland, a song composed for and dedicated to a
patron. Planxtys vary in time signature, and are usually
intended as listening pieces rather than dance music.

air- the melody of a song or march played as an instrumental
listening piece. Very often they are in 3/4 time. Airs
are played in a stately tempo.

waltz- in 3/4 time; the waltz was a popular 19th century
dance that entered the folk tradition. Waltzes are most
popular among American, Canadian and English fiddlers.

Understanding Fiddle Tunes

Almost all fiddle tunes have a similar structure. They
are divided into two or more parts, but usually two. Each
part is referred to alphabetically, the first part being
the "A" part, the second is the "B" part, and so forth.
Each part usually consists of either four or eight measures
played once and repeated. Sometimes the full eight or sixteen
measures are printed, to show how the part can be varied
the second time around. After eight or sixteen measures
are played, you move to the next part. The parts are sep-
arated by double bar lines. One reason why fiddle tunes
are so consistently structured is to allow the musician
(and the dancers) to know what to expect. If you are learning
a tune that you have never heard before, you can predict
when it will change parts.

Furthermore, you will notice that in any given tune, some
of the measures are identical. The same melodic idea presented
in the first four measures of a part may reappear, slightly
altered, in measures five-eight. Very often the cadences,
or end measures, of the different parts may be identical.
So when you play a tune for the first time, take a minute
to scan the music for similarities and repetitions. They will
help you learn the tune more quickly.

Combining Tunes

It has become customary in the British Isles and some parts
of America for fiddlers to combine two or three tunes into
a medley or "rake". Fiddlers that played for dancers had
to play for long times at a stretch, and changing tunes in
the middle of the dance made things more interesting.
Later, medleys were encouraged when fiddlers had to fill the
entire side of a 78 r.p.m. record.

You may wish to combine some of the tunes in this book.
There are three points to consider when doing so, listed
here in order of importance:

Type of tune- reels are usually combined with reels, jigs
with jigs, etc., although you may like to start with a slow
air or waltz and suddenly shift into a more spirited tune.
This can be very effective.

Key- the keys of the tunes should be related somehow in
order to gain a smooth transition; either the same, (G to G),
adjacent (G to A), relative minor or major (G to Em, Em to G),
or tonic to dominant (count five notes up, like G to D).

Melody- sometimes tunes have similar melodies or seem especially
compatable. Let your own taste and intuition help determine
which melodies go together.

A Note on Key Signatures

British and American fiddle music has roots that predate

our modern notions of "major" and "minor." You will notice

that some of the melodies do not "obey" their key signatures.

For example, Tom Billy's Jig is written with three sharps-

f♯, c♯ and g♯(our key of A maj.) but in fact all the g's

are naturaled. But to leave the g♯ out of the key signature

would imply that the tune was in D maj. (two sharps-f♯ and c♯)

which is definitly not the case. Therefore the author has

chosen to use full key signatures and then adjust the melody

where necessary with accidentals. Fiddle tunes which consis-

tently depart from the conventional key signature are said

to be modal.

The Rambling Pitchfork

This Irish tune is also known as <u>Lambert's</u> <u>Jig</u> or <u>The</u> <u>Fisherman's</u> <u>Widow</u>. Notice the flatted third note in measure twelve and the flatted seventh note in measure thirty. Flatted thirds and sevenths are called "blue notes" by American fiddlers. Both Irish and American fiddlers use them to alter the melody and create a more lonesome kind of sound.

Collier's Reel

Compare the triplets in measure five with the corresponding four eighth notes in measure one, to see how the variation was derived. The triplets are an expansion of the melodic idea in the first measure.

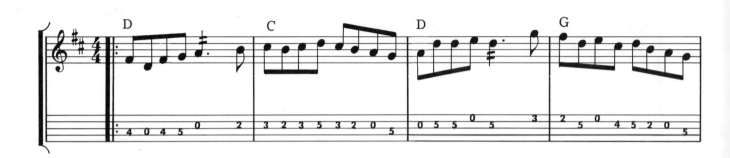

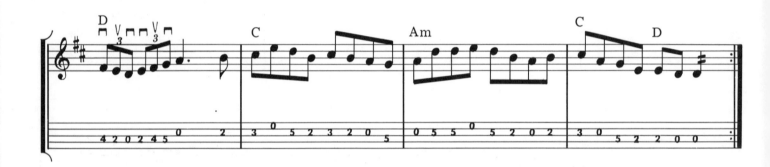

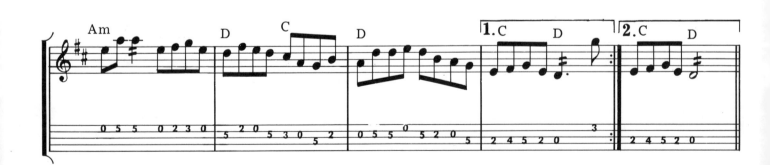

Green Grow the Rushes-O

A simple but hypnotic reel from Ireland. The "harp effect" works well in the "B" part.

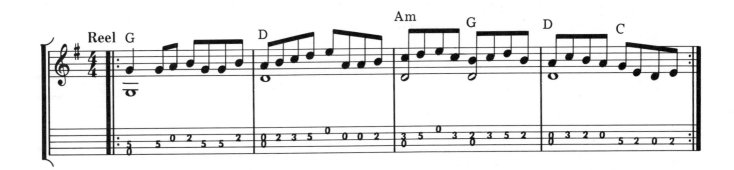

Jaybird

The "A" and "B" part repetitions have been written out to show some variations in the basic melody. After you learn some of the other tunes in the book, you might wish to add your own variations to them. Just be sure that you always play the original melody first, so that your listeners know what tune you are playing.

Jaybird is an American reel.

Mullingar Races

This tune was recorded as a duet by Paddy Killoran and Paddy Sweeney, two great Irish fiddlers, about fifty years ago. Mullingar is a town in the Irish midlands.

Weavin' Way

From Scotland via the Southern Appalachians.

The Trip to Durrow

A favorite of Irish pipers. The Trip to Durrow should be played fast.

27

The Huntsman's Hornpipe

The <u>Huntsman's</u> belongs to the great body of traditional fiddle music composed in nineteenth-century America. Many of these tunes would serve well as fingering exercises, and their melodies are often merely segments of scales and repeated left-hand patterns.

O'Donnell's Hornpipe

It appears that hornpipes were once much more popular among Irish players than they are today. Nineteenth-century collections contain hundreds of hornpipes that are never heard anymore. Perhaps the demise of the music halls in the United States, where Irish music and dance were nurtured, accounts for the disappearance of these fine tunes.

29

Rosin the Beau ♪

Here's a tune in the crosspicking style. You will find these left hand positions useful:

for measures
3,4,22,23

for measures
12,13

for measures
14,15

30

Hardiman the Fiddler

Slip jigs are hypnotic in their simplicity. It is thought that the 9/8 meter was much more common in ancient times.

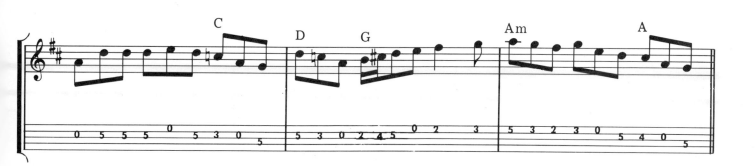

Forked Deer

An old time hoedown from the Appalachians.

Bumper Squire Jones

Planxties are sometimes referred to as set dances, to differentiate them from jigs. They were composed on the harp, and often do not conform to a predictable structure, because of the lyrical manner in which the Irish harp was played. Jigs, on the other hand, follow a predictable structure. Very often a planxty will be altered slightly to conform to the predictable jig structure, as in this version of Bumper Squire Jones. This planxty was composed by Turlough O'Carolan, the great blind Irish harper, who died in 1738. O'Carolan had ties with Baroque composers on the continent; you may discern this influence in the melody of Bumper Squire Jones.

College Hornpipe

The <u>College</u> <u>Hornpipe</u>, or <u>Sailor's</u> <u>Hornpipe</u>, was widely played prior to 1800 and continues to be a favorite. It occasionally appears in the key of D major, but B♭ major is the preferred key. One of the nice things about playing in the key of B♭ is that the seventh scale degree, a very important note in most fiddle melodies, (a in the key of B♭), is an open string and thus readily accessible. The same idea works in the key of F too; simply lift your first finger off the f note on the first string, first fret, and you have the open e leading tone.

The Mooncoin Jig

Mooncoin is situated on the River Suir in southern Ireland.

35

The Mooncoin Reel

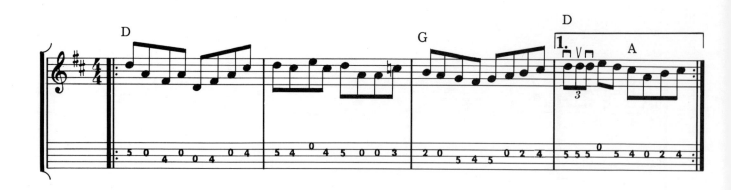

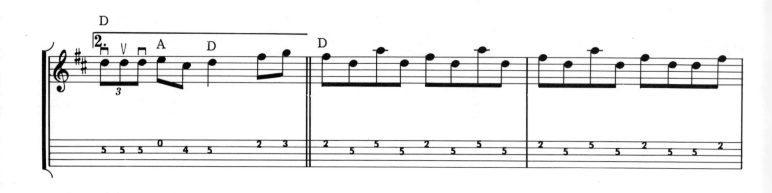

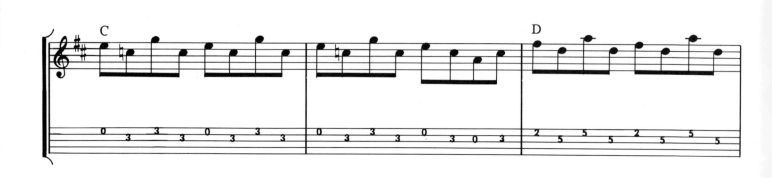

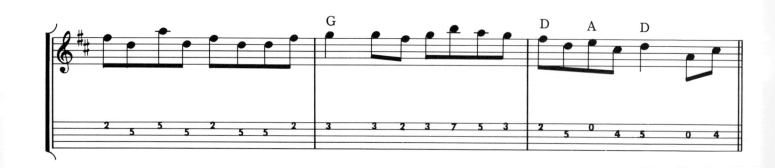

St. Anne's Reel

A lively Canadian tune. The chord progression in <u>St. Anne's</u> is unusual in that it utilizes the II (Em) chord. Don't be afraid to use your little finger in measure 13!

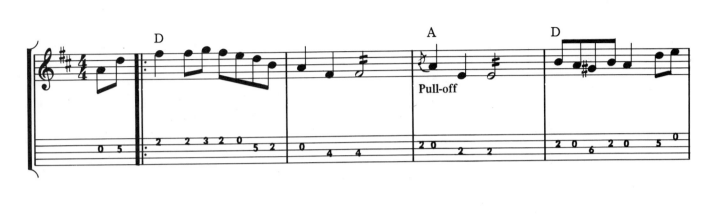

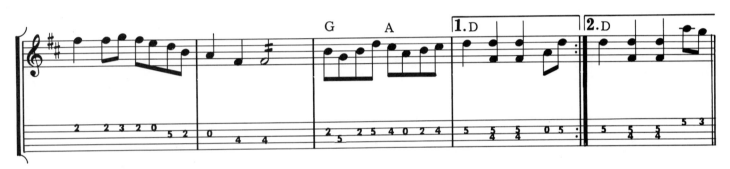

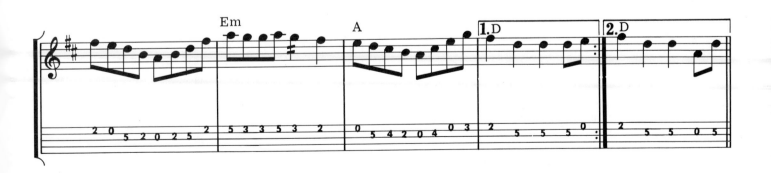

37

Off She Goes

The exchange of musical ideas between English and Irish musicians has been considerable down through the centuries. Particularly in Elizabethan times, Irish folk music enjoyed tremendous popularity in the English courts. Several fine jigs, Like Off She Goes, have come from England, despite the fact that the jig is usually associated with Ireland.

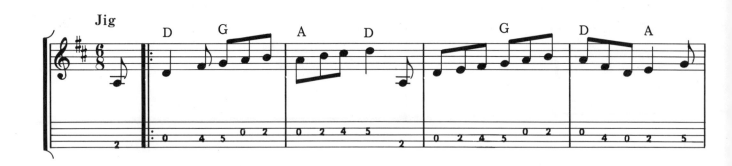

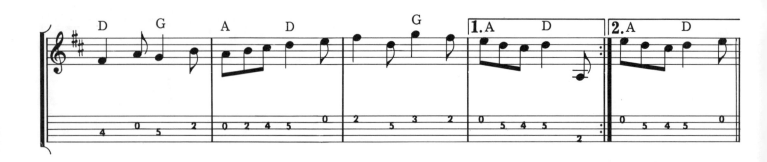

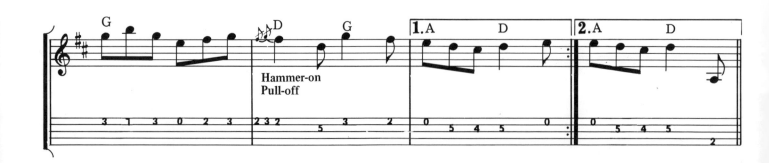

Brian Boru's March

Brian Boru was High King of Ireland and a Celtic hero; he drove the Vikings out of Ireland in the year 1014. A harp which reputedly belonged to him now rests among Ireland's national treasures. Play this one not too fast.

39

Nancy

Here's a straightforward tune that can be heard at New England contra dances. The simple melody and lack of ornamentation suggest that <u>Nancy</u> might have come from England.

Too Young to Marry

Also known as <u>Sweet</u> <u>Sixteen</u>, this tune is from the Southern Appalachians.

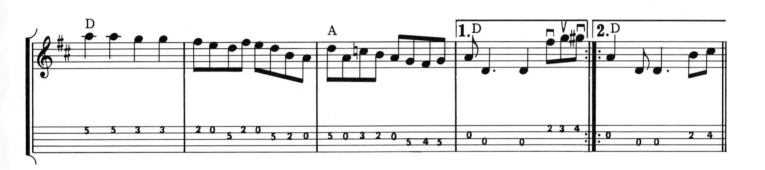

Thompson's Reel

This rarely-heard modal tune has some beautiful chord changes. The modal nature and flowing quality of Thompson's suggest that it comes from County Galway, Ireland. You will need to shift so that your first finger is at the third fret in order to play the "B" part.

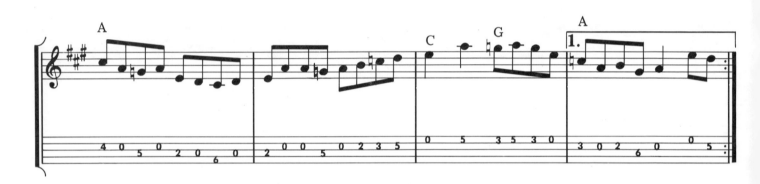

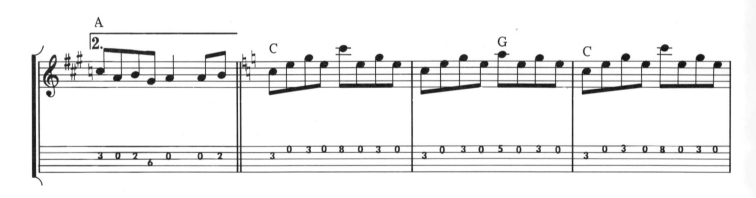

Thompson's Jig

Almost all fiddle tunes are in one of four keys: D, A, G, or C major. In these keys the fiddler can rely on open strings, which makes playing much easier. Occasionally a tune will appear in F major or Bb major. Thompson's Jig is played in F major, and it works very nicely. Thompson's is a Scottish jig which comes from Cape Breton, Nova Scotia, where authentic Scottish fiddle music continues to flourish.

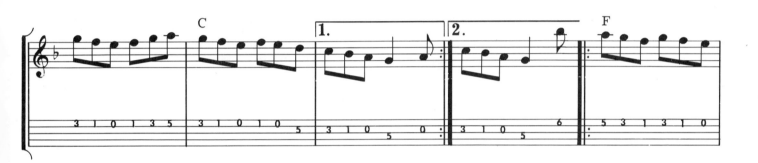

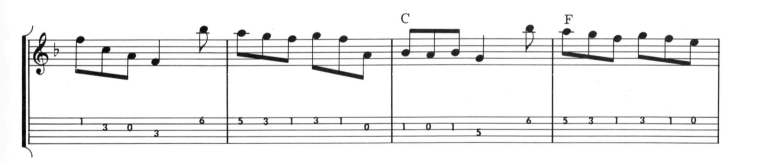

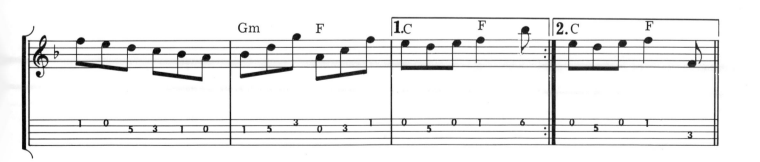

Spotted Pony

From the Oklahoma-Texas repertory.

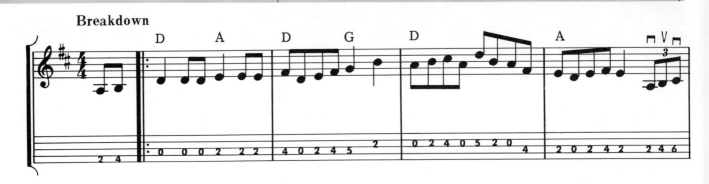

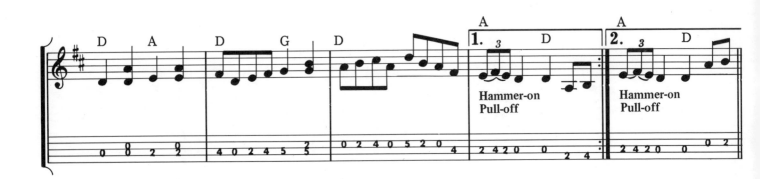

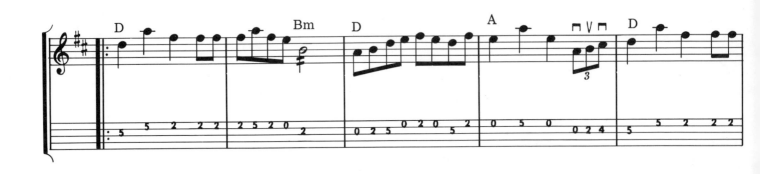

The Skye Boat Song

Here is a crosspicked version of a Scottish air. Play this one slowly. Try each measure by itself first, in order to discover the necessary left hand positions.

Stirling Castle

The dotted rhythms in measure 1, 2, 5 and 6 are a Scottish trademark, often referred to as the "Scotch snap". You will find it helpful to bar the third and fourth strings with your first finger at the second fret in measures 2 and 6. Concentrate on the triplets; play them cleanly and rapidly.

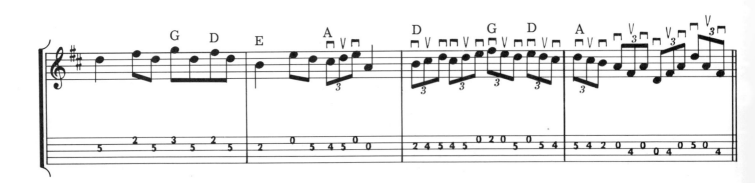

Rabbit in the Pea Patch

Uncle Dave Macon, the dynamic banjoist and entertainer, recorded this one around 1930. Uncle Dave's style of comedy and banjo playing reflects a lot of minstrel influence, and <u>Rabbit</u> <u>in</u> <u>the</u> <u>Pea</u> <u>Patch</u> probably came from the minstrel shows.

Breakdown

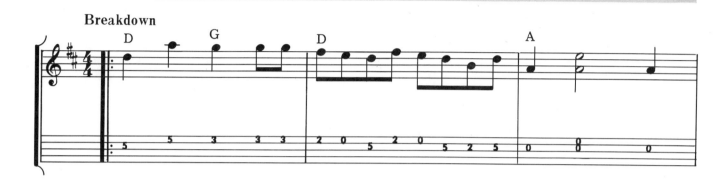

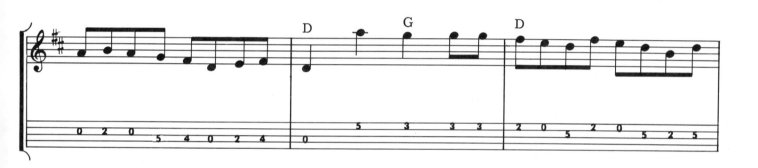

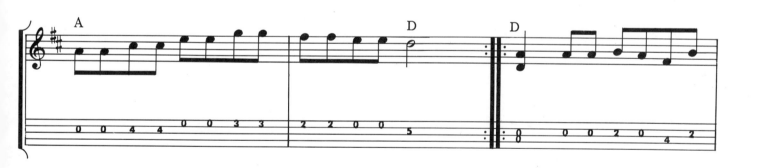

The Star of County Down

The Star of County Down is the Irish waltz version of a very common and widespread ballad melody of English origin. A number of ballad texts and songs are sung to this tune, including John Barleycorn, Dives and Lazarus and Brigg Fair. Sometimes the melody appears in 4/4 time. Pay close attention to the tremolo marks. In this tune, the absence of tremolo creates interest.

Pigtown Fling

This Irish reel is widespread in the U.S. where it is known variously as <u>Wild Horse</u>, <u>Stoney Point</u>, <u>Buck</u> <u>Creek</u> <u>Girls</u>, <u>Goin'</u> <u>Up</u> <u>Caney</u>, or <u>Old</u> <u>Dad</u>. It is customary to play the "B" part of this tune without a repitition. Notice that the first note in measure 1 is sounded with an up stroke, to accomodate the picked triplet that preceeds it. Try to play this one with a bouncy feeling.

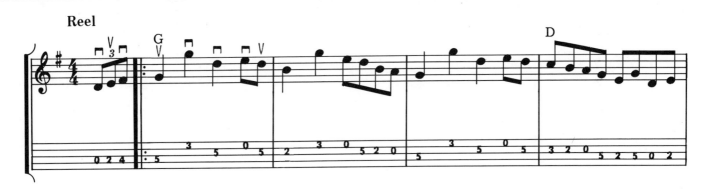

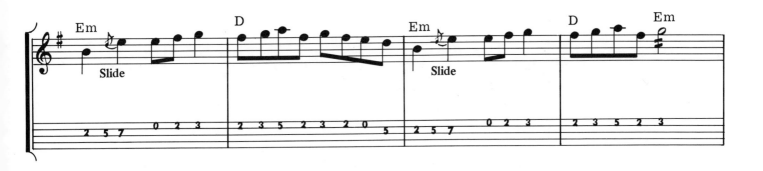

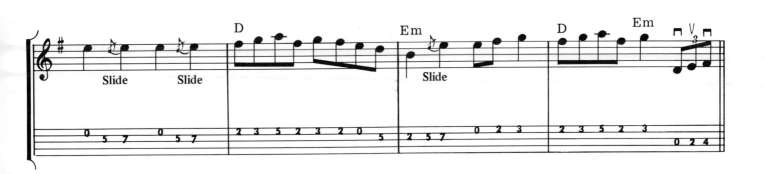

Hop High Ladies

Don't let those high notes scare you away from this beautiful tune. The half-note double stop at the end of measure 6 will give you enough time to shift your left hand. With your first finger at the fifth fret you will be able to reach the high notes. Hop High Ladies, also called Miss McLeod's Reel, is Scottish in origin.

Limerock

Limerock is played as a contest piece in fiddle competitions in the southwest, and as you might expect, it is very demanding and requires alot of left hand shifting. I've heard the parts of this tune played in different orders, so you might wish to do it differently. Limerock is classified here as a hornpipe, though in fact it sounds more like a polka. The tune may reflect some influence from the large numbers of East Europeans that settled in parts of Texas.

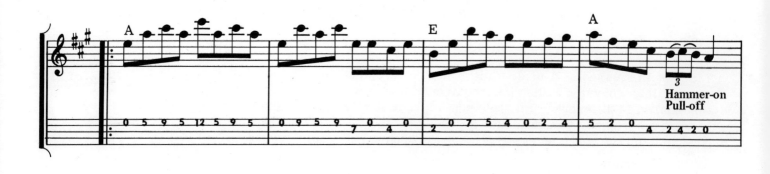

Tobin's Jig

<u>Tobin's</u> or <u>Tobin's</u> <u>Favorite</u> is a fairly common Irish jig that lends itself well to variation when played at a moderate tempo.

The Banks of Red Roses

This pleasant little melody does little to suggest the nature of the text that is often sung to it, in which the protagonist murders his girlfriend on the banks of red roses.

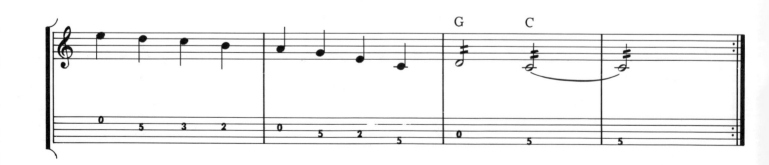

Old Mother Flanagan

This tune is heard most often in the southern Appalachians, though doubtless it is of Irish ancestry. The unexpected C chord in the "B" part is particularly interesting.

Toss The Feathers #1

<u>Toss the Feathers</u> is an unusual tune. Like many Irish reels, it appears in several variants, but the variants of <u>Toss the Feathers</u> are markedly different from one another. Two variants are presented here. <u>Toss the Feathers #1</u> requires that you bar the second and third strings at the second fret, in measures 1, 2 and 3. Both variants contain pull-offs which you should practice separately before you attempt the tunes. These two variants can be played as a medley.

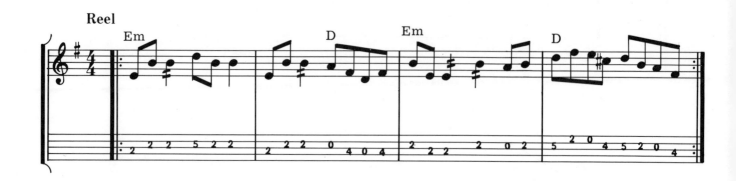

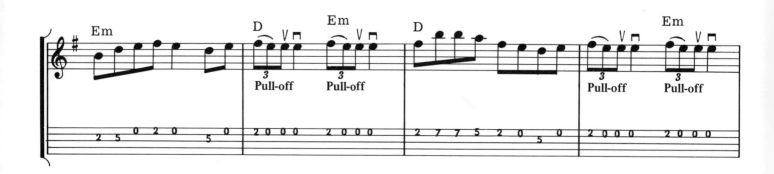

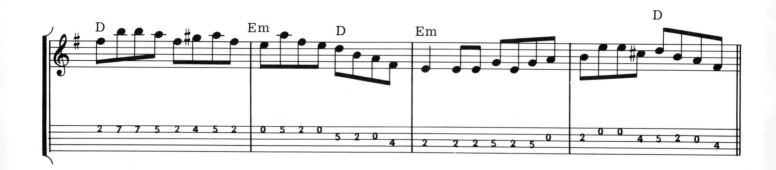

Toss The Feathers #2

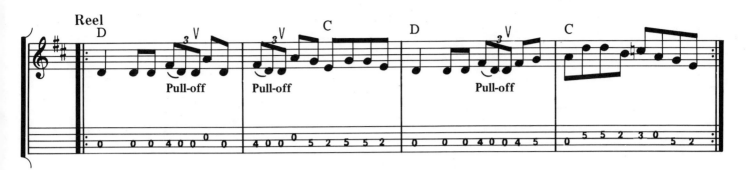

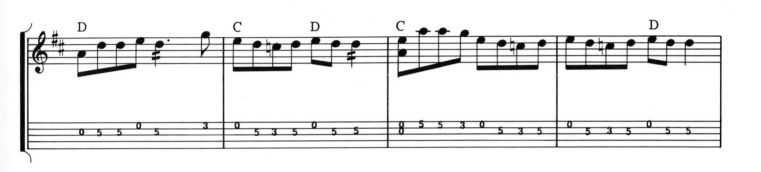

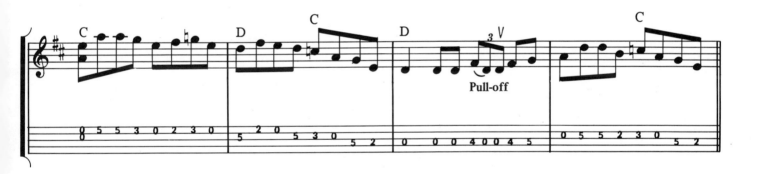

Richmond

Richmond is a showpiece for southeastern fiddlers and may be from the Civil War era.

Jockey to the Fair

Jockey to the Fair comes from England, where it is used to accompany Morris dancers. It has an uncomplicated scale-like melody but a well-developed chord progression, and it is played in F major. Altogether, an unusual tune.

The Handsome Cabin Boy

This melody is borrowed from an English song in which a young woman dresses in man's attire and signs aboard ship as a cabin boy. An interesting story...

Texas Quickstep

The hammer-ons connecting measures 1-2 and 5-6 must be done very hard in order to imply the beginning of the new measure. The last two measures require a strong fourth finger; here's the left hand position you'll want to use:

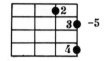

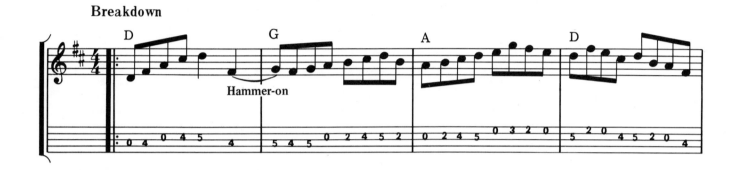

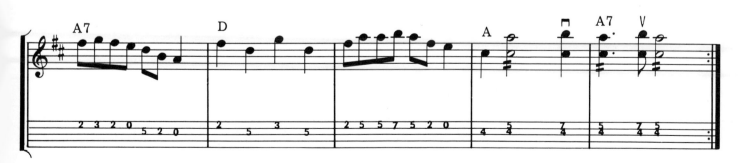

61

Texas Gales

I learned <u>Texas Gales</u> from a West Virginia fiddler in New Jersey. Good tunes have a way of getting around.

Boys of Blue Hill

A common hornpipe, ideal for stepdancing. Don't forget to linger a bit on the odd-numbered eighth notes.

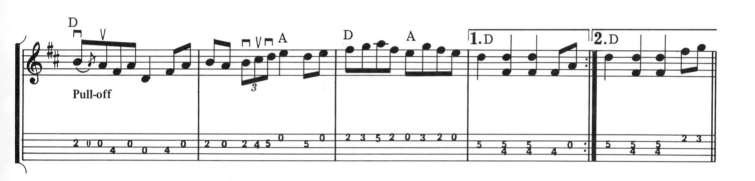

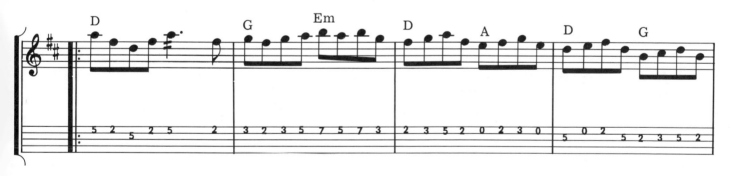

Greenfields of America

An estimated one million people fled repression and famine in Ireland in the mid-1800's, most of them bound for the "green fields of America". This reel was popularized by a 20th-century immigrant, the great Sligo fiddler Michael Coleman. It sounds best when played fast. Using the fourth finger on the seventh fret, second string (measures 1 and 5) will help increase your speed.

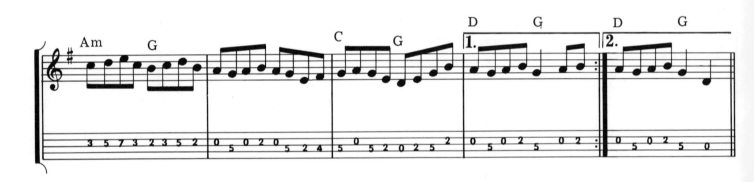

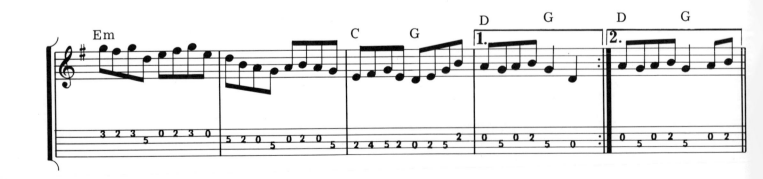

Timour the Tartar

Timour the Tartar was recorded in 1910 by the great Scottish fiddler J. Scott Skinner. Skinner was a colorful character. Known as "the Strathspey King", as an octagenarian he represented Scotland in Henry Ford's Lewiston, Maine fiddling competition of 1926. Like many of the better Scots fiddlers, his technique was classical in its refinement, yet the Highland tunes were Skinner's passion. Play this one in the Scottish manner; that is, at not too great a speed.

65

Tom Billy's Jig

County Kerry, in the extreme west of Ireland, has retained much of the ancient Gaelic language and culture once found throughout the British Isles. Kerry tunes, such as Tom Billy's Jig, seem to preserve some of the primitive wildness associated with the Celtic people.

Over the Waterfall

Here's a tune that's popular with fiddlers in the northern United States. Practice the double stops separately first, so when you get to them in the tune they will be familiar. Notice that the "A" part is repeated an octave higher-this is a nice way to vary a tune in the key of D.

Moloney's Wife

Play this tune briskly. The rapid back-and-forth picking on the sixteenth notes (measures fifteen, nineteen and twenty-three) will require a bit of concentration. Be sure to try this one with guitar or piano accompaniment; the chord changes in the "B" part are especially moving!

Dusty Miller

This modal Scottish reel is a favorite of Texas-style contest fiddlers. It should be played fast.

Lark in the Morning

Several folk tales exist which explain the title of this spirited Irish jig. My favorite goes like this: A town's two best fiddlers were bitter rivals, each one claiming to be the better musician. It was decided one evening that they would have a competition to prove who was the best in town. They began exchanging tunes around sunset and the contest wore on through the night. Each tune was played faster and more furiously than the one before. Finally, at the crack of dawn, a lark's song was heard above the fiddlers' din. The two men were humbled by the beauty of this natural song; they proclaimed the lark to be the winner of the contest, and they be came fast friends.

70

The Blackthorn Stick

Measure nine would make a great left hand exercise all by itself, but you won't want to ignore the rest of this tune. It was recorded by Michael Coleman in the 1920's or 30's.

March of the King of Leix

Leix (pronounced "Lay-sh") is a county in central Ireland. Marches like this one are of very ancient origin, and were originally harp pieces. This was composed in the 1500's for Rory O'Moore, chieftain of a powerful Irish clan. Play this tune slowly, with the solemnity befitting a king.

Un Homme Marie

The French-speaking Cajuns of southwestern Louisiana are descended from French Canadians who fled Acadia after the British gained control of their lands in 1755. They have maintained their traditional music and have influenced American country music to some extent. The typical Cajun band consists of one or two fiddles, accordion, guitar, and a triangle to keep the rhythm. Un Homme Marie, a Cajun waltz, should be played at a moderate tempo.

The Fisherman's Hornpipe

Also known as <u>Fisher's Hornpipe,</u> this tune is well known in Ireland and throughout America. Fiddlers in the southern and western U.S. play <u>The Fisherman's</u> more like a reel, that is, without the bouncy rhythm characteristic of a hornpipe. Try it both ways.

Boston Boy

Nineteenth century America produced some fine native hornpipes and reels. Boston Boy is typical of these, in that the melody is scale-like and rhythmically uniform. Native American reels are usually played in a driving tempo and without much ornamentation.

Fox Hunter's Jig

A captivating, yet simple, slip jig, Fox Hunter's is a favorite of Irish pipers, who will often imitate the barking of the hounds on their Uillean pipes. There is an extra hesitation, marked by the dotted value, on the first note of most of the measures. This adds a bit more of an eccentric bounce.

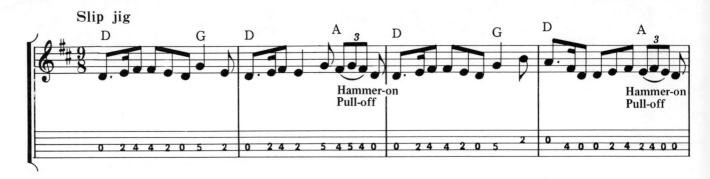

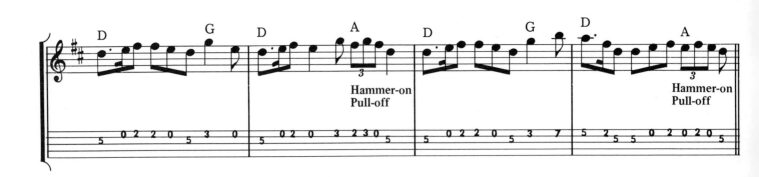

Ladies on the Steamboat

Before the Civil War, travelling black-face minstrel shows were the main form of popular entertainment in the U.S. Quite a few American fiddle tunes originated from the minstrels and remained popular with rural players. Ladies on the Steamboat is one such tune.

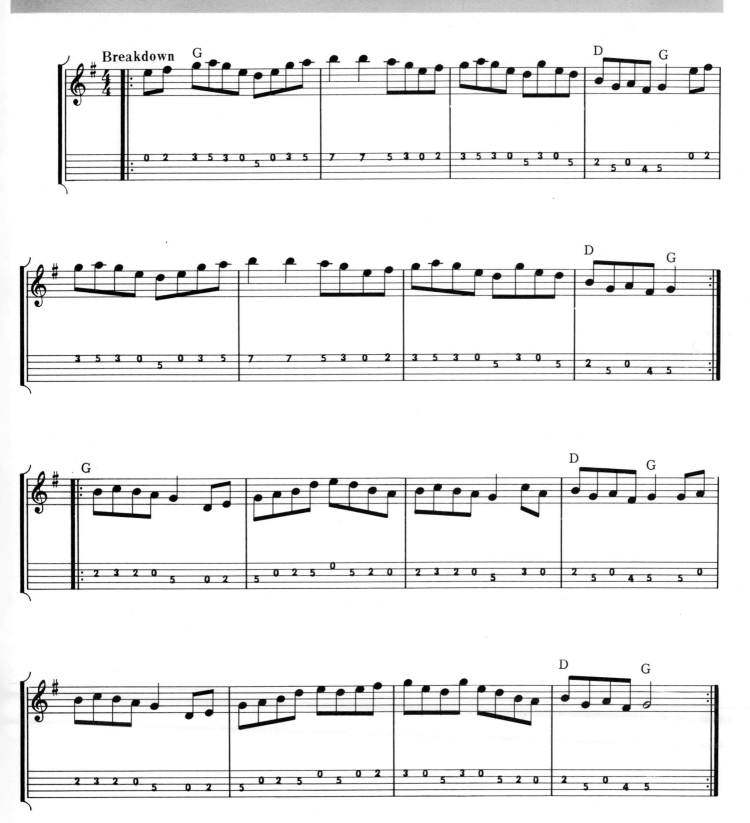

The Newlywed's Reel

The Newlywed's is a French-Canadian tune. The French-speaking area of Canada has produced a number of fine fiddlers and tunes, and there is a lot of exchange between the French and Scots -Irish traditions in Canada and New England.

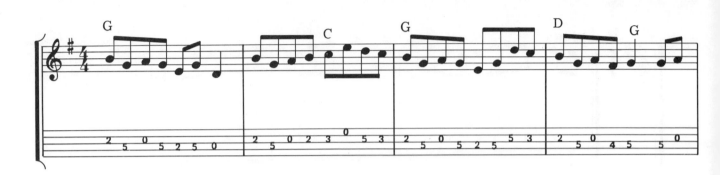

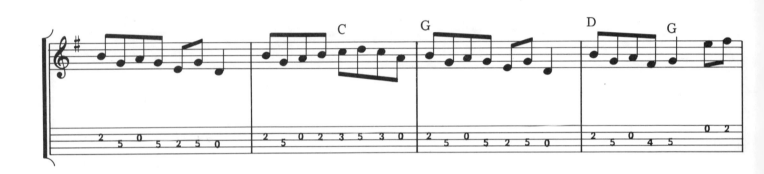

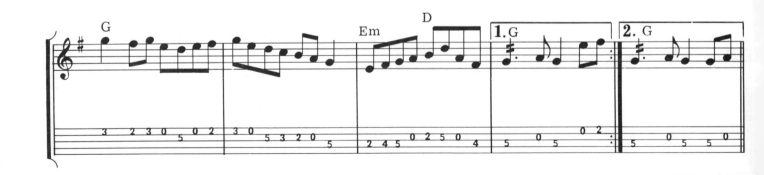

Drowsy Maggie

Drowsy Maggie is well-known on both sides of the Atlantic. The change from minor to major key helps create a feeling of tension and release in this tune. As in Toss the Feathers #1, it is helpful to bar the second and third strings at the second fret in the first three measures.

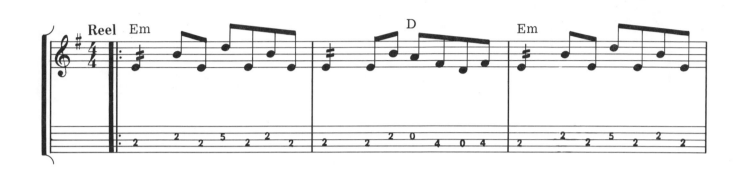

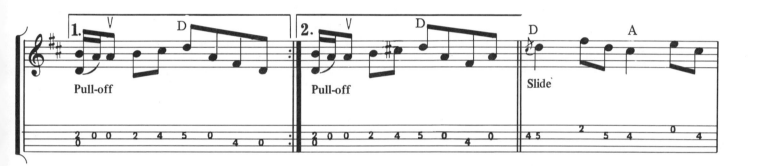

Byrne's Hornpipe

Be sure to play the e note of the picked triplet in measures 8, 9, 17, and 18 with your fourth finger. This is a technique that fiddlers use a lot; it makes for a smoother-sounding triplet.

College Groves

College Groves is an Irish tune which also goes by the names Cottage Groves and The New Demesne. It is a close relative of the reels Jenny's Welcome to Charlie and Jenny Picking Cockles. The hammer-on-pull-off motif in measure 4 is tricky and reoccurs throughout the tune, so you might want to master this idea before attempting the entire piece. You can pick, rather than hammer, the triplet notes in measures 16 and 24 if you desire. Be aware that the c notes in the "D" part are sharped, making the "D" part major rather than modal. The "E" part is minor. This kind of modal-major-minor alteration creates a great feeling of tension and release.

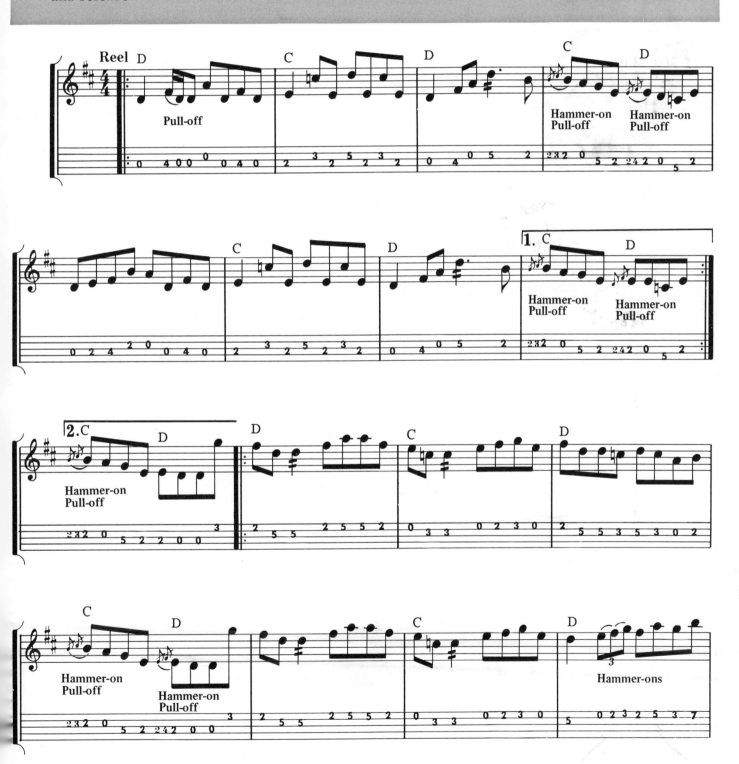

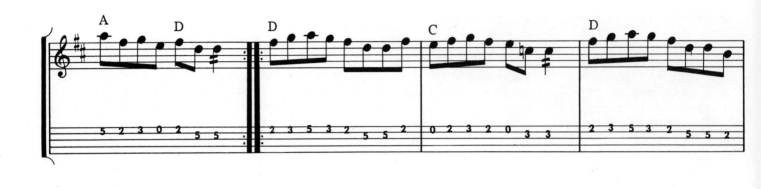

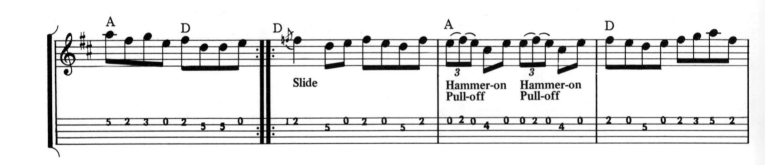

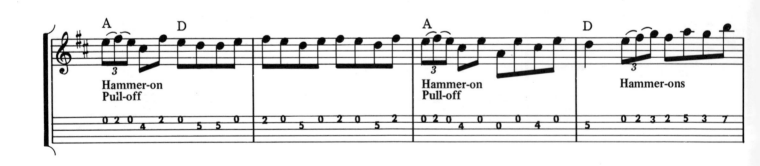

Cowboy Waltz

This is the kind of waltz you would hear between sets at a western square dance.

Harvest Home

A well-known Irish hornpipe, very similar to the American tune called <u>Fred</u> <u>Wilson's</u> <u>Clog</u>.

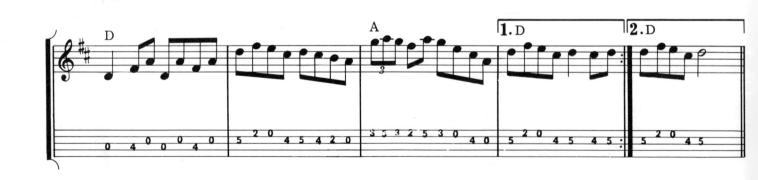

Chord Charts

Here are some recommended chord forms for accompanying the preceding tunes. Each chord appears in two forms, an "open" form for brush chords on the left, and a "closed" form for chop chords on the right. You are encouraged to seek alternatives to these recommended forms.
X - Do not play this open string   0 - play this open string

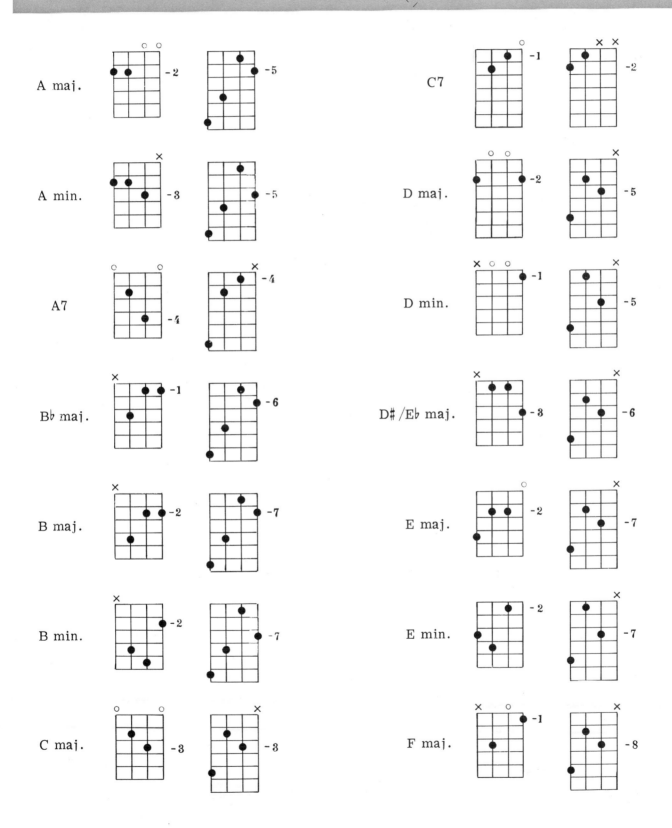

85

Chord Charts

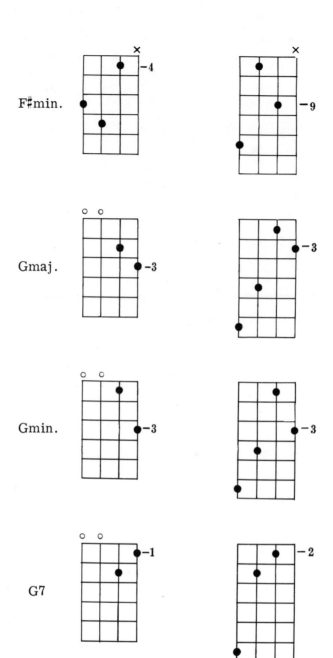

Discography

The following record albums contain examples of the tunes in this book. A variety of performers, styles and instruments is represented. You will find that these recorded versions are often quite different from the arrangements in the book, and only a few of the albums actually contain mandolin. Nevertheless, the records will help you gain a feeling for playing and adapting fiddle tunes and Irish music.

Each entry is numbered; check the discographic references in the index to see which album contains each tune.

1. Matt Molloy, Paul Brady, Tommy Peoples. Mulligan LUN 017.
2. Irish Dance Music. Folkways FW 8821.
3. Eric Thompson, Bluegrass Guitar. Kicking Mule KM215.
4. Kathleen Collins. Shanachie 29002.
5. Mick Moloney. Green Linnet SIF 1010.
6. John Vesey and Paul Brady. Shanachie 29006.
7. Kevin Burke, Sweeney's Dream. Folkways FW 8876.
8. Dave Swarbrick, Swarbrick. Transatlantic TRA 337.
9. J. Scott Skinner, The Strathspey King. Topic 12T280.
10. The Chieftains 2. Island ILPS 9365.
11. The Chieftains 3. Island ILPS 9379.
12. The Chieftains, Bonaparte's Retreat. Island ILPS 9432.
13. The Dillards with Byron Berline, Pickin' and Fiddlin'. Elektra EKL 285.
14. The New Lost City Ramblers, String Band Instrumentals. Folkways FA 2492.
15. Fennig's All-Stars, Saturday Night in the Provinces. Front Hall FHR-05.
16. Denis Murphy and Julia Clifford, The Star Above the Garter. Claddagh CC5.
17. The Red Clay Ramblers, Merchants Lunch. Flying Fish 005.
18. The Drones and the Chanters. Claddagh CC11.
19. Blue Ridge Barn Dance. County 746.
20. Uncle Dave Macon, Early Recordings. County 521.
21. Red Rector, Appaloosa. Old Homestead OHS 90044.
22. Byron Berline, Dad's Favorites. Rounder 0100.
23. Larry McNeely. Flying Fish 3320.

24. Pigtown Fling. Green Linnet SIF 1019.
25. Steeleye Span, Now We Are Six. Chrysalis CHR 1053.
26. Mike Seeger, Old Time Country Music. Folkways FA 2325.
27. Ernest V. Stoneman and His Dixie Mountaineers 1927-1928. Historical HLP 8004.
28. Bill Monroe's Uncle Pen. MCA DL7-5348.
29. The Wheels of the World. Shanachie 33001.
30. The Tony Rice Unit, Manzanita. Rounder 0092.
31. Cajun Social Music. Folkways FA 2621.
32. Son of Morris On. Import IMP 1013.
33. Paddy Killoran's Back in Town. Shanachie 33003.
34. The Hotmud Family, Years in the Making. Vetco LP 513.
35. The Legacy of Michael Coleman. Shanachie 33002.
36. Rodney and Randy Miller, Castles in the Air. Fretless 119.
37. DeDanaan. Shanachie 79001.
38. Angus Chisholm, Early Recordings. Shanachie 14001.
39. Frankie Gavin and Alex Finn. Shanachie 29008.
40. The David Grisman Rounder Album. Rounder 0069.
41. Bill Monroe, Blue Grass Time. MCA 116.
42. The Boys of the Lough, Good Friends, Good Times. Philo PH1051,
43. Bob Black, Ladies on the Steamboat. Ridge Runner RRR0018.
44. Butch Robins, Forty Years Late. Rounder 0086.
45. Bill Monroe, Bluegrass Instrumentals. MCA 104.
46. Sweeney's Men 1968. Transatlantic TRA SAM 37.
47. Frank Wakefield. Rounder 0007.

Index of Titles

Everybody's Music Teacher